Looking Forward

Be a looker-forward and not a looker-back.
Be a presser-onward upon life's stony
track. Don't waste time regretting the
things you cannot mend. Anticipate good
fortune at every twist and bend.

Keep going, never doubting the outcome
of your dreams. Have faith in their
fulfilment. Though dark the future seems—
Believe that somewhere somehow God's
purpose will unfold—and the grey horizon
be turned to blue and gold.

Give thanks for every blessing, your job,
your home, your friends. Don't take these
things for granted. A grateful spirit lends—a
glory and a meaning to pathways drear and
dun. Expect a bright tomorrow and turn
towards the sun.

The Healing Years

Though all must suffer loss and grief—
Time is kind and brings relief . . . The
passing of the healing years—deadens pain
and dries the tears.

At first . . . hearts break and sorrow numbs.
No word consoles. No comfort comes . . .
But slowly to the quiet mind—Life flows
back for Time is kind.

The Turn of the Road

Life's a road, a road that seems to run on
smooth and straight—until it takes a turn
and you are face to face with Fate . . . You
thought you knew where you were going
when you made a start. You travelled on
quite gaily with a light and singing heart.

Soon or late you always reach a place where
you must take—an unexpected turning and
you have to make a break—with all the
old familiar ways, but as your way you
wind—you find that you have no regrets
for what you leave behind.

So when changes come along upsetting
present schemes—welcome the experience
though strange at first it seems . . . The
change that you so dread may be a boon
and prove to be—the most important
turning on your road of destiny.

A Dream at the End of the Day

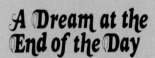

You never quite know where the road will go when you set out to follow a dream. You never can see what the end will be when you're caught in a magical beam— for dreaming can lead you right out of your senses—to walk in the path of a star. So if you're afraid of romance and adventure you'd better just stay where you are.

Few have the time to chase will-o-the-wisps. There is always so much to get through: the treadmill routine, home and garden to tend—meals to think of and shopping to do . . . But don't close your eyes to the light in the skies and the beauty that grows by the way. Keep a niche in your mind where you know you can find—a dream at the end of the day.

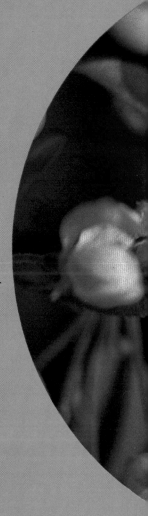

How Can You?

How can you cling to a grief that is old—
when blossoms are breaking all rosy and
gold . . . How can you hold to a sad old
regret—when Nature is saying,
Rejoice and forget.

How can you brood over things that went
wrong—when outside the window a
thrush makes a song? How can you think of
ill luck or mischance—when down in the
orchard the daffodils dance?

How can you fail to be glad in your heart—
when new buds are swelling and bursting
apart . . . How can you sit there and not
want to sing—your praise to the Lord for
the joy of the Spring.

The Way Out of the Wood

Don't give up and say that it's the end. Often at a time of crisis matters start to mend . . . It seems we have to reach a certain point before we see—the way out of the wood of trouble and adversity.

Things have to reach a climax. That's the way life seems to go. When they're at their worst that is the time for us to show—faith in God, believing that He leads us for our good—through the darkness, showing us the way out of the wood.

Sermons in Snowdrops

Wouldn't you think you were clever if you
found that you could make—something
as perfect as a snowdrop? Now the white
buds break—opening their petals,
forming bells that sway and swing.
Wouldn't you think you were smart if you
could make such a lovely thing?

Yet they come back every year—the same
yet ever new. It always thrills you when
the first green points come thrusting
through—but do you see them as the
working of a miracle—proof of One who
loves the world and makes it beautiful?
Things Divine are shown to us in little
ways expressed—messages from realms
of Spirit: hope made manifest.

Time Heals

One must go and one be left, the lonely
road to tread. There comes a day when all
must face the road that lies ahead—knowing
that the best is over with the loved one
gone—but Time is good. The passing years
their balm of healing bring, and like a
bird at Winter's end the heart begins to
sing.

We come at last to realise death breaks the
earthly tie—but Love survives when grief
has passed, for Love can never die.

Solo

Alone upon the leafless bough a blackbird
sang a song. The sky was grey and wintry
but his note was sweet and strong. No
company, encouragement or coaxing did
he need—no cue, no audience to applaud,
no prompting and no lead.

Alone he sang for pure delight and as I
listened there—There came the thought
that Love too sings where all is bleak and
bare—its nature to express in face of malice
and mistrust. Love, umprompted, gives
itself and sings because it must . . . meeting
the unspoken need with charity and grace—
like the bird that sings impromptu in a
lonely place.

Tomorrow's Door

Tomorrow is God's secret. I must not ask
to see—over the horizon where His hand is
leading me . . . Tomorrow's road is hidden
and I must be content—trusting in His
goodness; quiet and confident.

I must not try to question what lies beyond
today. Sufficient is the knowledge that I
can never stray—outside the bounds of
mercy. Whatever is in store—is where I
cannot see it: behind Tomorrow's door.

Towards the Sun

December is the dreary month that brings
the longest night, the deepest depths of
darkness and the shortest span of light.
But once the shortest day is over, changes
come about—week by week we see the
wintry twilight lengthen out.

So December's sombre cloak conceals a
lovely thing—the fledgling hope that
warms the spirit with a thought of Spring.
It brings the longest night, but ere the new
year has begun—it brings the shortest day
that turns the world towards the sun.

What You Were

When you think that everything is finished
think again. There is always something left.
Some vestige must remain—of what you
once believed you were and once again
can be: one who has the gift of fighting
back courageously.

When it seems you've failed in life don't
put your tools away—You will need them
yet for there will surely come a day—when
you want to set to work to make your world
anew. Next time you'll be stronger and a
little wiser too.

When you feel you've failed and lost the
best of everything—another chance is given
and you're heart begins to sing . . . Do not
miss the moment. Use the powers that you
possess—to build upon the ruins, turning
failure to success.

God Uses Broken Things

God can use a broken thing His meanings
to explain. The bursting mesh of Peter's
net that could not take the strain—of the
haul miraculous . . . And spikenard
outpoured—from Mary's broken box for
the anointing of the Lord.

Five small loaves were broken and a
multitude was fed. Still today He feeds us
with the sacramental bread—offered at the
altar. And to breaking hearts time brings—
the comfort of the knowledge that God uses
broken things.

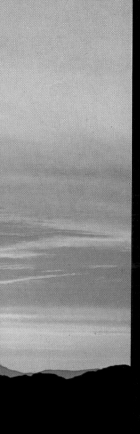

Under the Shadow of a Guiding Hand

We do not always see the way ahead. We do not always know which path to tread. This is the point at which we need to light the lamp of Faith to take into the night.

Trust and believe that God is leading you to a fulfilment hidden from your view. Know only good can come of what is planned, under the shadow of that guiding hand.

It is not always granted us to see—what lies behind the present mystery. Waste not words in asking why or where. Time will unfold the answer to your prayer.

Thoughts at Harvest-Time

How bored we grow with things that
human beings have designed. The scientists
perform their tricks, but do not stir the
mind. Yet we never lose the thrill of nature's
wonder-screen. The never failing magic of
an ever changing scene.

Many times we've watched the cornfields
turn from green to gold. The pattern is
familiar as the picture is unrolled—but
every time it happens it is strange and fresh
and new—Never does the eye grow weary
of the harvest view.

God's creations never bore. So wonderful
they are! The seed, the corn, the reaping.
Morning light and evening star . . . How
dull our own inventions seem, how feeble
and how small—beside the marvellous
design that lies behind it all.

Never Rest Content

Be contented with your life, but not with
how you live. Never rest content with
what you do and what you give. Always go
on trying to improve on yesterday—
brightening the path for someone else
along the way.

Be happy and be satisfied with what you
now possess—but never with yourself.
Be ever ready to confess—your faults and
failings. Grumble less and do a little more—
to make yourself a nicer person than you
were before.

Do not be too sure that all is right and well
with you. Keep on checking up on all you
think and say and do. Be contented even
though you've found no lucky star. Be
content with what you have, but not with
what you are.

One Year Younger

Do not mark the milestones as the path of
life you tread. Do not add the birthdays up
but count your friends instead. Count your
blessings one by one. You'll be surprised to
find—what a lot you can discover,
searching through your mind.

Do not measure time, but if you want a
sum to do—count the many mercies that
the Lord has granted you. Count the boons
and benefits, the things you're thankful
for. There's no ending to the list. There's
always something more.

When you feel you're growing older, don't
tot up the years. Look back and be thankful
as each milestone disappears. Count the
happy memories, the prizes and the plums—
and you'll feel one year younger every time
a birthday comes.